Animals from Head to Tail

COWS FROM HEAD TO TAIL

By Emmett Martin

Please visit our website, www.garethstevens.com. For a free color catalog of all our high-quality books, call toll free 1-800-542-2595 or fax 1-877-542-2596.

Library of Congress Cataloging-in-Publication Data

Names: Martin, Emmett, author.
Title: Cows from head to tail / Emmett Martin.
Description: New York : Gareth Stevens Publishing, [2021] | Series: Animals from head to tail | Includes index.
Identifiers: LCCN 2019043550 | ISBN 9781538255445 (library binding) | ISBN 9781538255421 (paperback) | ISBN 9781538255438 (6 pack) | ISBN 9781538255452 (ebook)
Subjects: LCSH: Cows–Juvenile literature.
Classification: LCC SF197.5 .M327 2021 | DDC 636.2–dc23
LC record available at https://lccn.loc.gov/2019043550

First Edition

Published in 2021 by
Gareth Stevens Publishing
111 East 14th Street, Suite 349
New York, NY 10003

Editor: Therese Shea
Designer: Laura Bowen

Photo credits: Cover, p. 1 Clara Bastian/Shutterstock.com; p. 5 Peter Cade/The Image Bank/Getty Images Plus/ Getty Images; p. 7 (top left) DaydreamsGirl/E+/Getty Images; p. 7 (top right) John Elk III/Lonely Planet Images/ Getty Images Plus/Getty Images; p. 7 (bottom left) burroblando/iStock/Getty Images Plus/Getty Images; p. 7 (bottom right) GUILLAUME SOUVANT/Contributor/AFP/Getty Images; pp. 9, 24 (horn) Patrick Shyu/Moment/ Getty Images; p. 11 Alexander Narraina/Shutterstock.com; p. 13 oxygen/Moment/Getty Images; p. 15 dejan_k/ Shutterstock.com; p. 17 Lester Lefkowitz/Photographer's Choice/Getty Images Plus/Getty Images; p. 19 Clara Bastian/iStock/Getty Images Plus/Getty Images; pp. 21, 24 (udder) Podulka/E+/Getty Images; pp. 23, 24 (calf) Canetti/iStock/Getty Images Plus/Getty Images.

Printed in the United States of America

CPSIA compliance information: Batch #CS20GS: For further information contact Gareth Stevens, New York, New York at 1-800-542-2595.

Contents

Female Cattle 4
Cow Bodies 6
Plant Eaters 16
Cow Milk 20
Calves 22
Words to Know 24
Index 24

Cows are cattle.
They are female.

Cows have hair.
They can be different colors.
Some have spots.

Some cows have horns.

A cow's eyes are on the sides of its head.

Cows can move one ear at a time!

Cows use their tail
to keep flies away!

Cows eat plants. Farmers give them food too.

Cows chew and swallow food. The food comes back up as cud. Cows eat cud!

Cows make milk.
It comes out their udders.

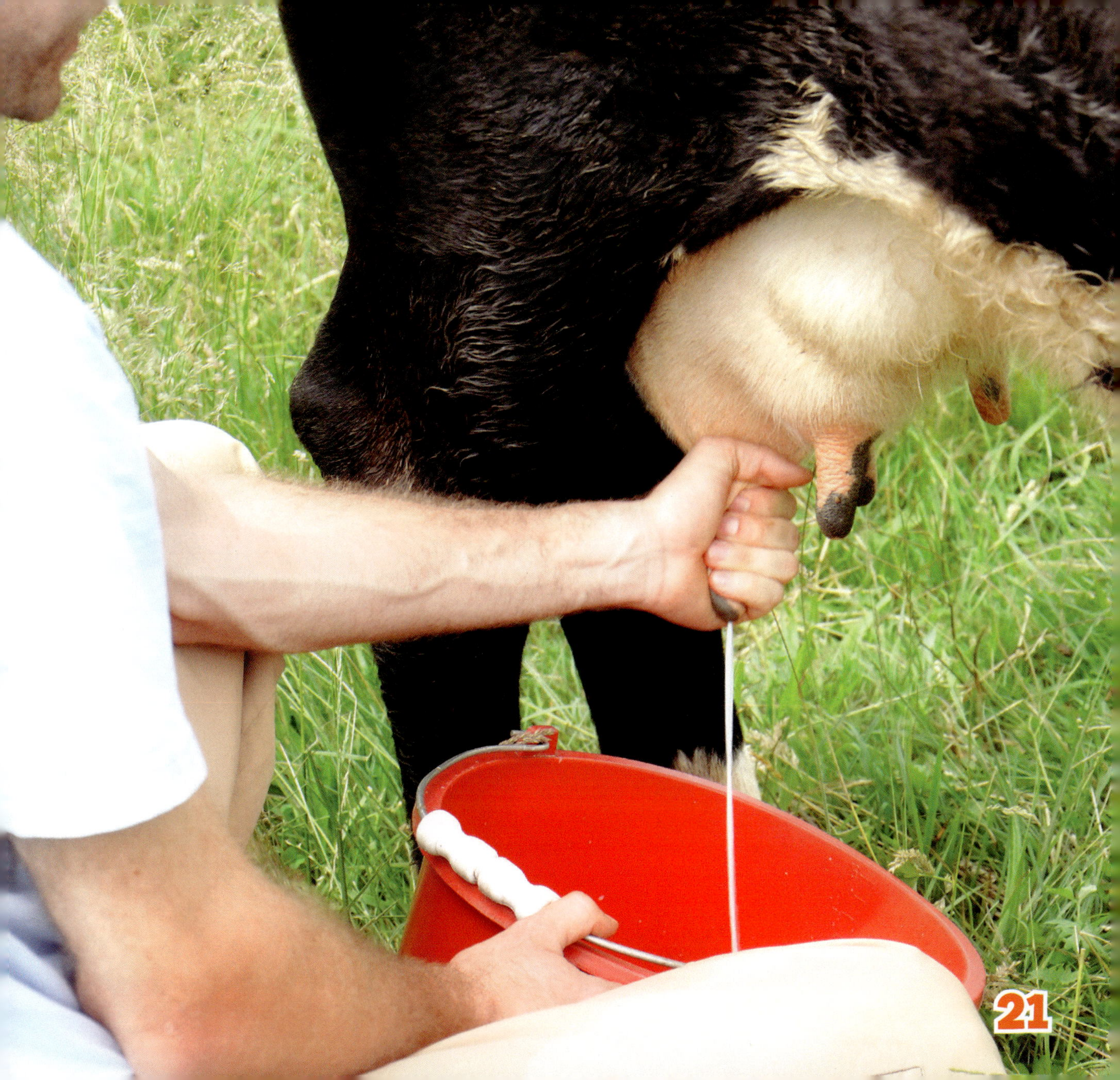

Cows have babies.
The babies are
called calves.

Words to Know

calf

horn

udder

Index

babies 22
cattle 4
cud 18
food 16
hair 6
milk 20